# JOHN BRIGGS' PARADISE

## *A Farcical Comedy*

Pierre Meunier

**Spectrum Books Limited**
Ibadan • Owerri • Kaduna • Lagos

Published by
Spectrum Books Limited
Sunshine House
Second Commercial Road
Oluyole Estate
PMB 5612
Ibadan, Nigeria

in association with
Safari Books (Export) Limited
Bel Royal House
Hilgrove Street
St. Helier
Jersey
Channel Islands
UK

ISBN 978 246 210  1


Printed and bound in Nigeria by Verity Printers Ltd., Ibadan

# Contents

iii

# Contents

# Foreword

It is rare and undoubtedly a streak of the genius for a non-theatre professional or practitioner to come up with a masterpiece, in the style of Jean-Baptiste Poquelin (1622-73) (Moliere), the great French playwright. *John Briggs' Paradise* manifests the qualities of a work designed by a maestro. After carefully reading the manuscript of this play, I discovered it to be sufficiently entertaining as a literary work of art even before that urge to realize it on stage which comes to a professional theatre director after a worthy literary excursion. It is no wonder then that by the time I was formally commissioned to direct the play the enthusiasm was already there.

Written in a very flamboyant and buoyant style, it begins to ascend the ladder of intensity of tempo, mood and tone from the very beginning until it explodes in a climactic resolution, effecting an effluxion of catharsis in the reader/audience. The playwright, naturally, without undue artificiality adhered to the conventional plot pattern of a well-designed dramatic work moving progressively from the exposition, traversing the complication to the resolution. This makes it a play worthy of academic study. What of the conspiracies, the asides, the soliloquys, the dramatic ironies including the engaging suspense and shocking but pleasant surprises?

The author captures the essence of the personality of Giovanni Jacopo Casanova de Seingalt (1725—1798) in the characters of John Briggs and Anthony Rowland. Tony represents the tempter, a fawner ever-willing to assist in committing dreadful sins of betrayal or disruptions, a depraved and perverted mind only likable to a gigolo in erotic exploits. In his 'finite' wisdom he leads John Briggs' through a labyrinthine full of pleasures and risks, himself coming out of it unscathed and unrelenting. Johnny's home and life would have been totally disrupted and destroyed if not for the large-mindedness of the women and a permissive culture.

John Briggs' transformation from a great conformist, quiet man-of-the-family to an hedonist who operates the philosophy of 'pleasure is the chief good' is effectively and dramatically handled. The author successfully depicts man as an adventurous, reckless, chauvinistic, lying,

v

fickle-minded dreamer, as against the painstaking, ever-gullible, naturally affectionate opposite sex. He captures man in his most restive state with great potentials for illogicalities and unprofitable escapades which sooner or later always culminate in a catastrophe. What does it profit our self-conceited men who leave the peace of a settled home to go after whoredom?

In language, tempo, tone, mood, dramatic action, plot and comic intensity, the play is enthralling. Pierre Meunier successfully gives a new dimension to the nuances of comedy — a veritable mix of all shades of comedy. Full of humour and not directly satirical, very realistic yet bordering on the fantastic.

Pierre Meunier is a humorist of great sensitivity, a man who relishes the task of making others laugh. He displays the idiosyncracies of a consummate writer of comedies. I have lately handled some of his other plays with more still in the offing. He is very prolific. I love the fact that he is a naturalized white Nigerian determined to draw his motifs from the Nigerian cultural milieu despite a glaring universal outlook. He produces works that are as relevant to theatre practitioners, as they are to anthropologists, sociologists as well as to the psychoanalyst who would not hesitate to think that the man is always reproducing himself in one of the characters in his play.

This work and others by Pierre Meunier would be very useful to the married as well as the unmarried, especially, to marriage counsellors. I shall tell you what it is like seeing, hearing or reading the play. At the end of it all, psychologically, you enter a state of Nirvana.


Bayo Oduneye
*The Director*
*The National Troupe of Nigeria,*
*Lagos*

# Preface

When I came to Nigeria more than forty years ago, I had no idea that I was ever going to take to writing as a profession. But as I savoured my new life in Africa I began more and more to feel that in the African setting in which I looked at everything from a double perspective, I had to set down my observations and experiences in black and white. Being French in origin I kept comparing everything I saw and experienced in the African setting with what I had seen and experienced in the western setting. And having known Africa, even the west acquired many new dimensions for me.

My 'seeing double', so to say, resulted in my being in a state of continuous excitement, impelling me to undertake a process of self-realization through the expression in words of my double vision.

At first I wrote only short stories and poems. But my imagination was so full of the dramas of real life that I took to writing plays as the only way in which I could picture to myself what I had seen and heard and reacted to among the many kinds of people I had the chance to operate for business or pleasure. So the dozen or so plays that I have written including *John Briggs' Paradise* are purported to be precisely such pictures.

What stands out conspicuously in my experience of African social, political and spiritual contexts is just such dramas. I thus look upon plays as a means of presenting dramatic conflicts of one sort or another. The conflict may be internal, external or both; within an individual, between two individuals, between an individual and a group, between two groups, or between a group and human society generally.

However, the conflict suited to expression in a play must be in or between humans, and/or between ideas, ideals, ideologies or attitudes. After all, it is under pressure from these that humans are swung into action beyond the activities of fulfilling their basic biological needs.

So in a play there must be people, there must be ideals and there must be action exactly as in real life. But a drama from real life cannot be photographically transferred to a play. The latter, within the space of a couple of hours and within the confines of a stationary stage, must present a sequence of actions that may span weeks, months or years. It may take place at a number of different places which could be far apart. It may be connected to numerous sets of actions that take other routes and lead to different conclusions. So, however close he may keep to the dramas of real life, a playwright has to edit, abridge, condense, give direction and shape, and expunge. At the same time he must bring out the point of view from which he looks at the happenings of real life. The point of view may crystallize as a moral vision approving or dissapproving certain kinds of attitudes or actions. That is how a play like any other genre of literature must be. Not only a picture of life, but a contemplation leading to a weighing of the pros and cons of undertaking or refusing to undertake a certain course of action.

*John's Briggs' Paradise* is meant to instruct as it delights. From the response that it has received from audiences in Nigeria—laughter and merriment combined with thoughtful musing—I gather that I have largely achieved what I set out to achieve. As to whether the play brings out the deeper springs of human psyche, it is obviously for the reader to tell.

I must herewith express my profound gratitude to the many producers, directors and actors who have done their utmost to make this as my other plays a resounding theatrical success.

# The Premiere Ensemble

## *The Cast & Crew*

| | | |
|---|---|---|
| John Briggs | — | Dele Adagunodo |
| Anthony Rowland | — | Sam Loco Efe (Snr.) |
| Angela Briggs | — | Nkechi Ezechi |
| Loretta Effiong | — | Vivian Ananaba |
| Madeleine Dickson | — | Emem Udofia |
| Man | — | Adeoye Bakre |
| | | |
| Play Director | — | Bayo Oduneye |
| Assistant Director | — | Bassey Effiong |

## *Production Staff*

| | | |
|---|---|---|
| Stage management | — | Adeoye Bakre |
| Costumes | — | July E. Undie |
| Set & lighting | — | Sunbo Marinho |
| Make-up | — | Mrs Felicia Mayford |
| Property manager | — | Adeoye Bakre |
| Production management | — | Da Costa Adeyemo |
| Business management | — | Oji Onoko |
| | — | Tony Okwuazu |

## *Technical Crew*

| | | |
|---|---|---|
| Technical Director | — | Sunbo Marinho |
| Assist. Tech. Director | — | Hillary Elemi |
| Set Construction | — | Ezekiel Agboola |
| | — | 'Biodun Abe |
| | — | Happy Ojadonor |

# CHARACTERS

**JOHN BRIGGS**    *(Johnny)*. Rich businessman, highly respected in Port Harcourt, his home town.

**ANGELA BRIGGS**    *(Angy)*. John Briggs' wife.

**LORETTA EFFIONG**    *(Lori)*. John Briggs' mistress who becomes his second wife.

**ANTHONY ROWLAND**    *(Tony)*. Johnny's friend.

**MADELEINE DICKSON**    Tony's friend.

# ACT I

## SCENE I

*The sitting room in John Briggs' house in Port Harcourt; comfortably furnished. His large-sized photograph is hung on the wall, flanked by that of his wife and his six children. The side-walls are covered with reproductions of portraits of saints.*

*The man passes, carrying a notice-board on which is written in big letters: PORT HARCOURT, 24 NOVEMBER.*

JOHNNY   *(to Anthony Rowland who is entering).* Hello Tony, how happy I am to see you! It's donkey's years since you last came here!

TONY   Oh yes, work Johnny, work and women!

JOHNNY   Oh yes, this damned work which makes us into slaves! And these damned women who also make slaves of us of another type!

TONY   But on both counts you are a privileged somebody!

JOHNNY   How?

TONY   You have a charming wife my dear. Younger than you, uncommonly pretty. She has given you six beautiful children, four boys and two girls.

JOHNNY   True. My children are delightful, my wife charming and my business going smoothly. Really, I have no reason to complain. Yet I try not to be their slave excessively. Inspite of all that... *(pause)*

TONY   Yes, yes. Go on, say what you have to say. What's on your mind?

JOHNNY   *(who goes to one of the two doors, half opens it, makes sure there is nobody behind and repeats the same thing at the second door).* Wait a minute so I can make sure we're alone.

TONY      Why all these conspiratorial manoeuvres?

JOHNNY    A little patience my dear. You'll soon understand. Only male ears can hear what I have to tell. And a friend's ears at that.

TONY      Then I'm your man. Being a man and being your friend.

JOHNNY    I don't doubt it, my dear. Everybody knows you to be a Don Juan, a Casanova, in short a lady-killer and a womanizer.

TONY      Is that all? Come on. Add more if you please. As for me, I'm listening. I'm all ears.

JOHNNY    Look my dear, I'm wilting in this orderly life. Cramped in the skimpy uniform of a husband. It's too tight and imprisoning. I am bursting with dance steps, bustling like a tempest, itching to move like a whirlwind. I am terribly fed up with having just one wife, and being a stay-at-home with so many women around to satisfy. I loathe my image of an austere man, who neither drinks alcohol nor smokes. I'm full of beans, my dear. I'd appreciate a goblet of champagne and a good cigar, any day, any time. Bloody hell!

TONY      I see, I see, Johnny, John Briggs, wishes to follow my way of life! To hell with ageing!

JOHNNY    *(flaring up)*. Oh yes, I've had enough of an orderly life! Enough of being a model father, a model husband, a paragon of virtue, a priggish moralizer, denouncing fornicators, downright drinkers, vicious fathers and faithless husbands.

TONY      I'm not surprised. I'm not surprised at all.

JOHNNY    Enough of carrying a big Bible under my arm for appearance sake when I go to church. My tastes are for a literature of a wholly different type and texture. And colour, if I may say so.

TONY      The colour should be blue, I guess. Right?

JOHNNY    Yes, rather. And enough of holding children on my knees, when I could hold some sweet little chicks as pretty as pictures and brazen enough to drive a saint crazy, on the same knees; *(pointing to the portraits of saints hung on the wall)* and enough of seeing always these portraits of saints scoffing at me!

TONY    I appreciate your problem my dear. It's what people call middle-aged lust.

JOHNNY  Middle-aged lust? I am too young for that.

TONY    A little before the due time perhaps. Well, midday and quarter to twelve are all the same. Forty or fifty years are all the same. It all depends on the man, you know.

JOHNNY  So my dear, what's your advice?

TONY    It's simple. Get a couple of mistresses. Or rather several.

JOHNNY  Mistresses?

TONY    Yes, mistresses. Not one, not two, but several, and certainly not in Port Harcourt.

JOHNNY  Yeah! I guess so.

TONY    Here you'll continue playing the peaceful father with your Bible under your arm and your children on your knees.

JOHNNY  What of the mistresses? Where shall I find them? Where shall I woo them?

TONY    In Lagos my dear. In Lagos, where you spend half of your time on business. From two weeks you could easily stretch it to three.

JOHNNY  How can I do that?

TONY    As a pretext you can say that your business is undergoing expansion.

JOHNNY  My dear Tony, you're suggesting outrageous remedies. Should my old lady hear you, she would claw your eyes out:

TONY    But she can't hear. So let's continue. Imagine yourself in Lagos for two to three weeks each month. Now there's no way to go up and down that frequently. It would only exhaust you physically and also exhaust your purse. Air fares are getting prohibitive and hotel bills are outrageously high. Rent a house in Lagos my dear friend, furnish it to your taste and live like a Nabob, hopping from one girl to another or taking a live-in-mistress who will act as a housewife.

JOHNNY      Your idea is super. I'll have two homes, two places of my own.

TONY        Oh yes, my dear, two homes! Fantastic, isn't it? You're going to live a double life and you'll see how thoroughly enjoyable it is. It's nothing but paradise on earth! *(they burst out laughing)*

JOHNNY      *(shaking with laughter).* And I'll keep a room for your use when I've found a house to rent or buy, since I want you to become one of the chosen few at my paradise.

TONY        The paradise of Johnny Briggs!
            *(they merrily laugh on)*

• • •

# ACT I

## SCENE II

*Angela Briggs joins them in the sitting room.*

ANGELA      *(who enters without knocking)* The more the merrier they say, so here I am! I heard you laughing right from the end of the garden. I must say that the garden is not very big, but even so... What's wrong with you? You're no longer laughing! My God, you bear a face as long as a fiddle, as though I'd caught you at something.

TONY        Hello Angy! *(he kisses her)* I am the cause of all that laughter. I was telling Johnny a funny story and he was laughing himself silly. I was seized by giggles at that. Laughter is contagious after all. When someone's fit of laughter ends, somebody else's fit of laughter starts.

JOHNNY His story sounded funny indeed. I have tears in my eyes.

ANGELA Tony, out with your story.

TONY *(who looks at Johnny smiling).* Oh no, it's for men's ears, not for women's!

ANGELA You are exaggerating. I'm no more a little girl.

TONY What's more if giggles get hold of us again and you add yours, we'll make the house tremble, blowing off the bloody roof.

JOHNNY Stop it Tony, my sides are tickled and giggles are climbing up my throat!

ANGELA All right! Keep your story and laugh in your sleeves. I'm going. *(from the door)* By the way Tony, be with us at Christmas.

TONY At Christmas? With the greatest pleasure.

JOHNNY Thanks indeed!

TONY I'll be with you, I promise.

ANGELA It's nice of you Tony. Bye, I'll see you one of these days. *(she goes out)*

. • .

# ACT 1

## SCENE III

*The same.*

JOHNNY Let's sit down. *(they sit in armchairs)*

TONY Johnny, I'll be your guest at Christmas, agreed. But on one condition. You must, before the new year eve, have your own house in Lagos, and on the same day have a house-warming party too. I'll be there to help you with a bevy of pretty girls. You'll be able to choose the one that pleases you most. You can have her on a trial basis, as both a mistress and a house-keeper.

JOHNNY     I assure you that's exactly what I intend to do.

TONY       That's the obvious result of our plans my dear.

JOHNNY     *(reflectively).* A life of luxury, that's what it is!

TONY       *(expansively).* Yes my prince, a life of luxury as if you were the lord of a manor, with a young princess gleaming on each of your knees, planting wholesome kisses on your lips.

JOHNNY     *(wistfully).* A life of luxury? What am I saying? Paradise on earth, with a crowd of houris with lips glued to mine.

TONY       Glued to your lips like leeches.

JOHNNY     Great! Fantastic! With a sweet murmur issuing from the same lips by way of music!

TONY       Not to speak of the superb dishes of all kinds and the divine beverages lined up before us within arms' reach.

JOHNNY     Marvellous! Splendid! You're equal to the occasion and so resourceful.

TONY       My prince, you really deserve this royal treatment. After the house-warming party your majesty will only have to give up being a model Dad and assume the burden of being a part-time bachelor.

JOHNNY     A part-time bachelor?

TONY       Oh yes! From time to time, periodically, you know, one day a married man, another day a bachelor.

JOHNNY     A periodic bachelor, I should say.

TONY       Exactly. Periodic. You've got the right word, once a bachelor, another time a married man, shuttling between purgatory and paradise, paradise and purgatory.

JOHNNY     *(who has trouble keeping from bursting out laughing).* Purga... Purgatory! Para ... Paradise? *(having a quiet laugh and going towards the door)* Let's see if Angy is around. *(opening the door and looking outside)* She must have gone to town, the car is no longer there.

TONY    Then let's make the most of it.

JOHNNY   Now I can laugh to my heart's content *(bursts out laughing)* and you too my dear Tony. Purgatory, paradise, I envy your ability to raise a laugh. When the missus is not around, the husband and his buddies can have a great time!

TONY    The great time will be all the greater with a little whisky and a lot of gin. *(bursts out laughing)*

JOHNNY   Straight away my dear Tony... of course I don't drink in public, but what's necessary for my friends and visitors I certainly have. *(going towards one of the sideboards, opening it and taking out two tumblers and two bottles which he puts on one of the small tables near each armchair)* Here is a glass, old chap, have whatever you want, whisky or gin, unless you prefer a bottle of beer.

TONY    Whisky!

JOHNNY   Gin for me. *(first serves Tony, then pours out two shots of gin for himself)*

TONY    My dear Johnny, toast to your new life! To your double life I should say and to your Lagosian home! *(raising his glass)*

JOHNNY   *(also raising his glass).* Where you'll be very welcome indeed!

• • •

# ACT 1

## SCENE IV

*Johnny Briggs' sitting-room at Port Harcourt. It's Christmas' eve. A man passes carrying a signboard on which is written in big letters: PORT HARCOURT 24/25 DECEMBER.*

*Johnny, Angela and Tony are seated around a big table on which there are lots of empty dishes and bottles.*

ANGELA    This Christmas eve dinner has been really great! The children were well-behaved throughout the midnight mass. Also during the meal that followed. Thinking of just one thing. The present which Father Christmas would bring them during the night.

JOHNNY    *(taking the Bible and opening it before him).* I thank God for having brought us together on this Christmas eve. May He grant us all peace and prosperity, Amen. *(they all make a sign of the cross)*

TONY      I am happy to be among you on such a beautiful day. It signifies a lot to me. I hope it will be followed by many others. *(winking at Johnny)* Be it here or elsewhere.

ANGELA    Tony, you will always be welcome. You are like a brother to us. Moreover, the influence you have on Johnny is beneficent indeed.

TONY      *(who has turned around to pick up the handkerchief he has deliberately dropped so as to face the public). (aside).* Me, a beneficent influence? *(laughing and grimacing)* It's rather evil, I guess. *(looking at Angela)* Thank you Angy, you are far too nice.

ANGELA    *(yawning).* Excuse me if I yawn. Not out of boredom, believe me, but fatigue. The preparation of a Christmas eve dinner is not a small affair. I'll leave the two of you to your discussions. Don't hesitate to laugh your heads off if you feel like it, since I'm going to sleep like a log. Good night my gentle lambs.

JOHNNY    Good night my angel, I won't be long in following.

TONY      And I won't be long in going, good night Angy, sweet dreams.

ANGELA    *(going out)* Good night!

• • •

# ACT 1

## SCENE V

*John Briggs' sitting room.*

JOHNNY     Now that we're only men, I must give you the latest news about Lagos.

TONY     Go on, I'm listening.

JOHNNY     I've got it! *(with a smile on his lips)* I've got it my dear!

TONY     But what?

JOHNNY     I've got the house!

TONY     The house? At Lagos?

JOHNNY     *(who nods)*. I've got it my dear Tony, and better still, at Ikoyi. Do you realize? The most posh area of Lagos!

TONY     At an affordable rent?

JOHNNY     Yes, indeed, and with the promise of sale my dear, can you imagine?

TONY     Terrific! You have the devil's own luck, Johnny old boy. So the house-warming party will be on. The 31st of December, eh?

JOHNNY     It's on, my dear. Everything's ready. I've all the furniture, all the dishes, all the drinks, you'll see. Now, it's your turn to play. The ball is in your court.

TONY     Well, you'll see which ball is the scorer. Above all, you'll see if my promises are empty. When you see me land with my bunch of girls on heat! Your head won't know which way to turn any more. I hope you understand what sort of head.

JOHNNY     *(bursting out laughing yet pretending not to have understood)*
           For pity's sake, spell it out for me.

TONY       No way. Be an ignoramus all your life. We'll fill ourselves up
           with food and fill the chicks up with, what do you think?

JOHNNY     Are you talking Greek or what? I don't understand a word.
           *(laughing to tears)* For goodness sake, spell it out for me!

TONY       Stop kidding, dear. With all this mob around you, on your
           knees and at your feet, you'll see how paradise is within your
           reach.

JOHNNY     How anxious am I to start my double life! One day with small
           brats on my knees and a glass of fruit juice in hand, another day
           with chicks on the same knees and a goblet of champagne in
           the same hand. Purgatory-paradise. Paradise-purgatory. Al-
           ternately, hyphen, period, hyphen; and what's great, without
           any visitation whatsoever to hell as a consequence.

TONY       One day with the Bible under your arm and the next with a
           magazine for well-informed adults.

JOHNNY     It is, I imagine, as if I would draw an imaginary line between
           Port Harcourt and Lagos. Whenever I cross the line I become
           another man. I'm born again. I change skin, mind and lan-
           guage!

TONY       That's just what it is, you're far from wrong.

JOHNNY     On one side of the line it's nothing but tedious sermons at
           soporific meetings of paragons of virtue, some more than
           others. In short, the monotonous and conventional life of a
           small provincial town.

TONY       And on the other it will be a stream of cocktails, choice
           dinners, dance-parties, visits to casinos and nightclubs. In
           short, the bright life of a capital, not to mention the wild parties
           to which your mistresses will drag you.

JOHNNY     Oh Tony, a change of life, a change of skin, what joy, even if
           it's only off and on. To move from one girl to another, like the

bee going from flower to flower, each day of the week having its own flower with a melodious name — Monday Yvonne ...

TONY     Tuesday Maggy!

JOHNNY   Wednesday Lola!

TONY     Thursday Sisi!

JOHNNY   Friday Tonye!

TONY     Saturday Frances!

JOHNNY   And Sunday Loretta!

TONY     O Loretta!

JOHNNY   Loretta the queen, just like Sunday the king of the days!

TONY     Congrats my dear, for that elegiac speech. Did the inspiration fall on your head, just like that, without a warning?

JOHNNY   From the sky to the corner of my heart. Without warning. Without notice. Exactly as you've just said. And the words sprang from my heart like bubbles!

TONY     How happy I am for you Johnny.

JOHNNY   I am grateful for that Tony. You've made me into another man. You've removed the blinkers that were blinding me. Now I see life as it should be, the way a free man should live.

TONY     Thanks Johnny, it's quite normal. Men must help one another, moreso since man, the male I mean, is by nature polygamous.

JOHNNY   Another truth which you've just expressed, my dear Tony. You're a real wise man. You should rewrite *The Rights of Man*, for the advantage of the males naturally. But let's leave these topics which are a bit too arid and let's talk about my new place in Lagos.

TONY     Go on, that topic interests me a lot, since I'm one of the chosen few of your paradise on earth.

JOHNNY   As you'll see in a few days' time, it is a big and beautiful double-storey house. The ground floor includes a big sitting-room, a dining-room of a respectable size, a gaming-room, a kitchen, a pantry, a garage and toilets. The first and second floor, include four bedrooms each, each self-contained with bathrooms and toilets. If I substract the guest-rooms, your own, they will house seven rooms. Can you imagine, seven! I can change rooms each day of the week or lodge in them a whole harem.

TONY    Well, you're doing alright for yourself. It's a prince's palace you have rented.

JOHNNY    Rented, yes, but with the promise of it being sold to me. I have the option to buy within six months.

TONY    A palace of a thousand and one nights! How did you furnish it?

JOHNNY    The sitting-room is almost identical to the one here. The nature and the arrangement of the furniture are the same. I have my habits you know and as such I don't risk going wrong, be it in Port Harcourt or in Lagos.

TONY    And the bedrooms?

JOHNNY    Each one is a jewel decorated differently. You will see your own, room number 8, as being out of this world!

TONY    All good and well, it's time to go. I'll see you again in Lagos er... at Ikoyi.

JOHNNY    Ikoyi, that's it ... Write down the address without indicating my name naturally. I had no complimentary cards printed, as I'm supposed to be living in a hotel! 1201 Bourdillon Road, Ikoyi. Tel. 50.401.

TONY    I'll be there on the thirtieth of December at 7 p.m. to get to know the place. I'll finalize the burial of your life of a doting father as well as the house-warming arrangements. That's not too far away. It's the 25th already.

JOHNNY     Not too far away, not too far away, you say! You're a funny one. Five days! That's too long! Believe me I am anxious to pass from purgatory to paradise.

TONY     A little patience, my friend, you'll soon have your little chicks. Come on, CIAO! *(going towards the door)* See you soon! *(he leaves)*

JOHNNY     Ciao!

*(the curtain falls)*

## ACT II

### SCENE 1

*Sitting room of Johnny at Lagos, identical to that of Port Harcourt but instead of pictures of saints, there are pictures of nude girls fixed on the wall, opposite his own picture.*

*Johnny is alone. A man passes carrying a signboard on which is written in big letters: LAGOS, 30 DECEMBER.*

JOHNNY    *(taking stock of his briefcase).* This briefcase belongs to John Briggs, a well-groomed young man and good father, the man of Port Harcourt. And I am John Briggs. Moreover here are the pictures of my wife and of my six children. Oh, look at my missal full of holy pictures, my cheque-book from a bank in Port Harcourt, my address book, the official one I mean, in short all the things which concern the known face of my life, the well-lit one! That one, my dear Johnny, is exposed on this very picture. *(staring fixedly at it)* We're all there, my six children, my wife and I. *(with tenderness)* It's not that I don't love you. On the contrary, I adore you, but I am bored to death with the narrow life in which I feel imprisoned, tied up, gagged. The boredom is too heavy to bear. It weighs me down, and crushes me. This other life which I'll soon start right here tomorrow will help me overcome this boredom which is oppressing me. *(spouting)* Goodbye boredom, goodbye melancholy! *(He sings)*

> Welcome gaiety, welcome smiles!
> Hello gaiety!
> Hello Songs!
> My life is a perpetual spring
> and I'm as happy as a lark.

> From now on my ideal shall be summed up thus:
> 'Love, drink and sing', a well-known slogan since the world

began.
*(pensively)* 'Love, drink and sing',
what a slogan, what a chorus!
I feel as though I had wings growing.
 *(humming)* Hello gaiety.
 Hello songs ...

   • • •

# ACT II

## SCENE II

*John Briggs' house in Lagos.*

TONY *(noiselessly enters on tiptoe and sits in a chair without Johnny noticing) (to himself).* Well, our man is happy this morning. We're far from the man in Port Harcourt *(pointing to the pictures of naked girls pinned on the walls)* and far from the portraits of saints hung on the walls of his home in Port Harcourt.

JOHNNY *(who turns and sees Tony).* Ah, there you are! I didn't hear you coming. I was doing some tidying up as you can see. I soon realized that I needed two briefcases, one for my stay in Port Harcourt and the other for my stay here.

TONY That's well thought. The briefcase is a good basis for the double life, believe me. In one, you stuff everything legal, family pictures, missal, address book and so on. In the other, pictures of your mistresses, concubines and girlfriends, in short, anybody in skirt who is not your wife, erotic books, membership cards of several bachelor clubs and a whole lot of other things. A good piece of advice, don't ever mix up the brief cases when you're going from one home to the other, that would be catastrophic.

JOHNNY    How shall I keep them? I can't of course have the two of them at the same time.

TONY      Certainly not! Mistresses are even more jealous than the wives, believe me. A woman is a woman and there's no one or nothing more jealous than a woman I swear, except maybe the tigress and it's yet to be proven.

JOHNNY    So what am I to do?

JOHNNY    It's very simple, you must find a place to keep the briefcase which you don't need ... of the good father and husband when you are in Lagos and of the merry bachelor when you go to Port Harcourt. Maybe you should also change your clothes when going from one home to the other. The cloak of a family man, very orderly and sober, has little to do with that of a gallivanting gay dog.

JOHNNY    You'll surely find me someone to carry out this little operation. The quicker the better. As you can see, I have already bought the second briefcase!

TONY      I'll find that someone. Trust me and not later than this evening. What about your New year eve dinner. Is everything ready?

JOHNNY    Everything's ready my dear. The beer, six sorts, the wines, five different vintages, the spirits, six different kinds, without counting the fruit juices and the fizzy drinks for the light drinkers. As for the grubs, it will be super you'll see. There will be a terrific buffet with at least twenty assorted dishes.

TONY      Twenty different dishes! That will be great, fantastic!

JOHNNY    Wait a minute, don't forget the dessert, which will total ten.

TONY      Fantastic! Great! Ten desserts, twenty different dishes, but that's a King's feast! Already my mouth is watering.

JOHNNY    And have you passed in review, your crown of girls?

TONY      Yes indeed! I did a complete inspection my dear, arms inspection and kit inspection.

JOHNNY    Arms inspection, kit inspection! What does that mean? Are the girls carrying guns?

TONY      Come on Johnny, a little imagination! With what arms are women abundantly provided? And what kit could I be talking about if not all the jewels, fineries and ingenious devices those ladies use to make themselves look beautiful!

JOHNNY    Oh you! You are a born joker!

TONY      It's good to laugh, isn't it? Would you want me to look a real misery on the eve of such a beautiful day?

JOHNNY    *(laughing)* Not at all. I prefer laughing myself silly to crying my eyes out.

TONY      Talking about girls, there's one coming to visit me soon. That will give you an idea of the kind of judies who will fall into your arms tomorrow night.

JOHNNY    A judy? What's that again?

TONY      Oh, nothing much my dear! Oh, you sure have just come out of your bush! A hopeless provincial man, a thoroughgoing country bumpkin, that's what you are. Judy, that's just another word for a girl, my dear Johnny. *(the door bell rings)* Well, well, I bet you it's her, Madeleine, the Judy I was talking about! *(singing to himself)* Madeleine, my dear Madeleine .... You relieve us of a lot of bother! *(to Johnny who cannot make up his mind to open the door)* Are you going to open or not?

JOHNNY    I don't know the girl.

TONY      Are you in your house or not? Moreover, maybe it's not her. If it's her that's the best way for you two to meet!

JOHNNY    *(acting like a little boy)* I am just shy you know, I'm not the lady-killer that you are!

TONY      Don't be scared, you'll soon be used to it. A few months of this way of life and you will beat me hands down in my own field! *(the ringing gets louder)*

JOHNNY    *(going towards the door)* I'm going ... *(laughing and swelling himself up)* And the judy had better behave herself!

· · ·

# ACT II

## SCENE III

*John Briggs' sitting room in Lagos.*

JOHNNY    *(opens the door and talks to the visitor at the doorstep)* *(shyly)* Oh yes Miss, it's right here. Oh yes, please come in!

MADELEINE    *(noticing Tony).* Ah, Tony you are here! *(enters a young and beautiful girl, smartly dressed)* I'm very happy. I was scared it was one of your practical jokes. *(looking around her)* Say, it's great in here! *(low to Tony)* and your friend looks quite friendly.

TONY    *(low to Madeleine).* He is very friendly as you'll get the chance to see, and timid but you must excuse him. It's his first extra-marital affair! *(aloud)* Johnny let me introduce Madeleine, a very good friend, extremely nice. She'll join us at your party tomorrow night.

JOHNNY    *(shyly).* Delighted to meet you Miss Madeleine. *(they shake hands)*

MADELEINE    *(gripping his hand tight)* Just Madeleine or Mado, if you don't mind. Leave off the Miss.

TONY    And to you Madeleine, I have the great pleasure and honour to introduce Johnny Briggs' a long-time friend!

MADELEINE    *(with a smile on her lips, still holding his hand tight)* Delighted to meet you Mr. Johnny Briggs.

TONY          Come on Johnny boy! *(pushing him in the back)* come on!

JOHNNY        *(overcoming his shyness).* Please drop off the Mister and my surname, just Johnny will do. *(letting go off her hand and opening his arms to her)* My dear Madeleine.

MADELEINE     *(falling into his arms).* My dear Johnny!

TONY          *(aside)* This is what they call love at first sight or I don't know anything about love. But how will he react, poor thing, when he meets Loretta tomorrow, Loretta who is twice as beautiful as Madeleine and who is attractive a score of times.

JOHNNY        *(kisses Madeleine in small greedy kisses on the mouth) (in between two kisses).* O treasure of my days and delight of my nights! O you Madeleine, my Madeleine!

MADELEINE     O Prince charming of my wildest dreams! You Johnny, my Johnny *(who kisses her wildly on the mouth).* Come, take me to the land of marvels where we shall together conjugate like the sun and the moon ....

JOHNNY        The verb 'to love' *(lifting her off the ground, carrying her in his arms and going out with her)* applies to all the tenses and all the persons.

TONY          *(laughing).* True love at first sight has put them in a tearing hurry. Tomorrow we shall have a good laugh when the rest of the crowd shows up with Loretta at the head! Faced with so many charming girls, poor Johnny will be on the horns of a dilemma. Madeleine? Loretta? Judith? Mary? Which one will he take as a mistress? He can't bring himself to choose between so many good looking wenches. It won't be long before it ends in a free-for-all. *(laughing even louder)* Oh dear! I can see fun in sight in *(gesturing)* boxing, wrestling, catch-as-catch-can, Judo, Karate! Ouch! Ouch!! Ouch!!!

• • •

# ACT II

## SCENE IV

*A man passes with a signboard showing LAGOS, 1ST OF JANUARY 5.00 A.M. Tony and Johnny are on scene. Johnny has a girl on each knee. Many empty bottles lie scattered on the floor.*

TONY          Johnny, your party was splendid, great, fantastic! There's no superlative adequate enough to describe it.

JOHNNY        *(makes signs that he is not in a position to reply). (Between two passionate kisses)*. Excuse me, my dear, I am very busy and I can't bring myself to choose between Mado and Lori.

TONY          The choice is difficult I admit, but it is necessary that you make up your mind. Anyhow, your party was super. The musicians and the singing girl were first class. You were not the only one to spray banknotes on their foreheads. Hats off, Johnny, we have ended the old year and started the new one in a blaze of glory! It's five in the morning, the last guests have just left, some staggering, some almost crawling on the floor. We are now only the four of us. I'll retire to my room.

JOHNNY        Stay a bit longer, will you?

LORETTA       Tony, do not go yet. It's me Johnny loves.

MADELEINE     Oh no, it's me!

LORETTA       It's you Johnny loves? *(rushing towards Madeleine)* Repeat that and you'll see.

MADELEINE     Just try to hit me and you will soon realize your mistake.

TONY          Come on girls! Come on, my darlings, be nice and gentle. Do like Judith and Mary who left without making any noise.

JOHNNY        *(low to Tony)*. There's a hitch here, but what to do?

TONY          *(low to Johnny)*. Let me choose since you cannot make up your mind. *(holding Madeleine by the waist and giving her a kiss)* Come on Mado, come with me, be reasonable! You had your turn yesterday evening, let Loretta have hers now.

Our friend can judge afterwards.

MADELEINE  Tony, it's because of you I'm dropping off. Let's go. Take me with you. No doubt, you're the best.

LORETTA  *(embracing Johnny tenderly)* Good night, both of you. No hard feelings.

TONY  *(going with Madeleine).* Good night! Good night! No hard feelings!

MADELEINE  *(holding Tony by the neck).* Good night! *(low)* I'll have my revenge, Johnny wouldn't get off lightly when I get hold of him.

JOHNNY  Good night, lovebirds. *(they go out)*

• • •

# ACT II

## SCENE V

*The Same.*

LORETTA  *(becomes very tender and loving)* Oh my love, I love you like nobody ever did.

JOHNNY  I feel the same darling.

LORETTA  *(passionately)* Our lovestory shall be sublime I will be yours, body and soul, and we shall be one.

JOHNNY  *(inflamed).* Come Lori, I am anxious to have our bodies become one. I can hardly wait to reach with you the supreme pleasure. *(dragging her in a state of great excitement)* Come, my love!

LORETTA  *(ecstatic).* Yes, my angel, oh, the supreme pleasure with you... *(they go out)*

*(the Curtain falls)*

## ACT III

### SCENE 1

### *The Same.*

*A man carries a signboard showing LAGOS 1ST OF JANUARY 12.00
NOON. Tony and Madeleine enter soon after the man has left.*

TONY        Oh, it's noon already! The first noon of the new year. I wish
            you once again a happy new year *(kissing her)*. May all your
            desires and dreams come true!

MADELEINE   *(returning his kisses).* Happy New Year to you. As for my
            desires and dreams, I don't expect too much from life. That
            way I don't risk being disappointed.

TONY        Madeleine, you must excuse Johnny for yesterday night or
            rather for this morning. You know the poor fellow has been
            deprived of that thing for a long time, stuck between an over-
            possessive wife and a colourless environment.

MADELEINE   Excuse him? Me? Never! How? Does it matter to me that he
            has been deprived of that? I don't want to see him any longer.
            Let him stay with his Loretta if he finds her so beautiful. And
            let him stuff himself with that thing.

TONY        Come on, Madeleine. Don't be jealous.

MADELEINE   You know very well that a woman is jealous by nature.

TONY        And man is polygamous by nature.

MADELEINE   Agreed, but there are limits to boorishness. To pet and neck
            me heavily as he did this morning and paw the other slut at
            the same time, one does not do that. He had taken me to the
            brink...er... the brink of the abyss, only to drop me after. I say
            no to that! You don't lead that far an action you don't mean
            to conclude!

TONY    It's all my fault. Moreover Loretta is as jealous as a tigress. And she clings like a leech! Had we not gone out, you would have come to blows.

MADELEINE    Come to blows? You're putting it mildly. I am well-equipped to hit back, with teeth as sharp as razor blades and claws like those of a panther. The poor wretch would have had only pieces of ears and nose left and may be eyes out of their sockets, had you left me to deal with her.

TONY    Look Madeleine, he meant to pay homage to both of you for your beauty. On such a night, he could have led both of you to paradise. There need have been no rivalry and no fight.

MADELEINE    Too bad for me, too good for her! Let her have her Johnny all to herself. I don't like such sharing. As for him, he had better not come and cry in my bosom after he gets tired of that slut.

TONY    Mado, come on, don't stretch the matter so far.

MADELEINE    What! Do you know Tony that only trains have not run over the body of that whore?

TONY    Mado, darling, Mado!

MADELEINE    I better go, I've had more than enough of advice. You make me sick with trying to be neutral. So Ciao! See you next time.

TONY    Leaving without saying goodbye to them?

MADELEINE    Say goodbye to those two? Never! I don't want to see their ugly mugs again. CIAO, Tony, you are deep down a nice guy! *(going towards the door).* You know where to contact me if you want to see me. Bye-bye, CIAO, and no hard feelings.

TONY    No hard feelings darling. See you soon. *(she goes out)* *(shaking his head)* No hard feelings, she said ... My God!

•  •  •

## ACT III

### SCENE II

*The Same. John Briggs' House — Lagos*

TONY        *(laughing on seeing the title of the big book which he has just taken from the shelf and pointing it out to the spectators)* EROSRAMA ... that's the new Bible of the gentleman. You old devil, you're not yet bored! You're pretty far from the old and new testaments which you are consulting all the time when in Port Harcourt.

JOHNNY      *(distraught, with swollen eyes, hardly able to stand, appears on the door step).* Tony my dear, you sure didn't exaggerate? That girl, damn it, is no extinct volcano! I am on my knees and I can hardly put one foot before another. OOOOOh my, oh my! My mind has gone blank my dear Tony, It's crazy. If you knock gently on my head, it will sound hollow!

TONY        I warned you, didn't I? Loretta's a dynamite. She's Madeleine raised to the power two!

JOHNNY      To the power two you say? I would rather say to the power ten! Power she has, my god! Enough and to spare! I must have damned reserves not to be feeling impotent!

TONY        I told you, didn't I? So that chick pleases you?

JOHNNY      She does, my God! She does.

TONY        Then it's simple. Keep her on a steady basis.

JOHNNY      I mean to, my dear. She will furnish wonderfully the new home I've got.

TONY        As furniture, she is simply first class, believe me.

JOHNNY      A piece of furniture, very alive and cosy.

TONY        What's she doing, isn't she coming?

JOHNNY      She is sound asleep. Dead to the world, almost. Come and see how beautiful she looks. Quite an angel. So full of sweetness is her face. *(he half-opens the door and Tony glances into the room).*

TONY     Beautiful! No doubt about it, but her being an angel is another story. As soon as she opens an eye, the angel changes into a demon.

JOHNNY     She is transformed, that's all. Passing from one state to another. And it's the demon in her I love!

TONY     You don't say!

JOHNNY     *(closing the door).* Let's leave the sleeping angel to rest on her couch, and continue our conversation undisturbed. Tony, how about a cup of coffee?

TONY     Great, my dear, that will wake me up!

JOHNNY     And me, my god! I'll go and prepare gallons of it. Strong enough to wake up a dead man. I am almost dead too, believe me, murdered, assassinated by whom you well know! *(he goes to the kitchen)*

TONY     *(alone).* He is crazy about her, the poor bastard. It's as plain as the nose on his face. Their affair will last long. I know them both.

• • •

# ACT III

## SCENE III

*The Same. John Briggs' sitting room — Lagos*

LORETTA     *(poking her head through the door).* Hello Tony! Where's Johnny?

TONY     In the kitchen, preparing coffee.

LORETTA     A very good idea he has had. I'll put on my dressing gown and come in. *(she closes the door)*

TONY      Yet another one with blue rings under her eyes! O love, physical or not, when you get hold of us!

JOHNNY      *(enters with a tray laden with a pot of hot coffee, cups, saucers and a sugar bowl).* Here my dear, a salutary drug for us all!

LORETTA      *(enters dressed in a filmy negligee).* Salutary and most welcome.

JOHNNY      *(putting the tray down and pouring the coffee in cups).* Come let's drink. It can only do us good.

LORETTA      What a pleasant aroma!

TONY      *(sipping his coffee as a connoisseur).* Pleasant indeed! That's just what any doctor should prescribe! Johnny is surely an expert in preparing coffee, real good coffee and not a foul brew! *(they drink in silence)*

LORETTA      Sudden silence! An angel is around, some may say!

TONY      Would he condescend to descend on us?

JOHNNY      I don't care. I have my angel already. *(coming close to Loretta)* Let him go! *(cuddling her)* One is more than enough for me! *(he kisses her and Loretta returns his kiss)*

TONY      *(melting and looking at them).* Go on, lovers. I must leave you alone to start the year with a flourish. I'll come around in a few days.

JOHNNY      *(still cuddling Loretta).* Don't go like that Tony. Stay on and have lunch with us. Yesterday's left-overs are there in plenty. *(thinking)* Where is Madeleine by the way?

TONY      Mado! It's donkey's years since she left, sorely disappointed.

JOHNNY      Disappointed? *(giving Loretta a kiss)* Sorely disappointed?

TONY      Of course! In very unflattering terms she declared she would never set foot here again!

LORETTA      *(giving Johnny a kiss).* That's just like Madeleine. She is downright jealous, because you prefer me to her.

JOHNNY     Well, I can't love two women at the same time. It would be a case of bigamy. And I don't care to be a bigamist.

TONY     *(who has a job keeping a straight face)*. Exactly! You can't afford that. *(to himself)*. A lawful wife in Port Harcourt and now one in Lagos, though this time not so lawful. And yet he is not a bigamist. Anyhow if he takes a third one, it will no longer be bigamy... *(thinking)* What's the word? *(asking the public)* Gamy-something, but what?

*(Somebody in the public)*. Polygamy!

TONY     Oh yes, polygamy!

JOHNNY     I can't even contemplate it.

LORETTA     Not at all! One wife, one man, that's the rule. Boy, that's the rule.

TONY     Ok, love birds, I'm off. By the way, Johnny, when are you going to Port Harcourt on business?

JOHNNY     *(surprised)*. Business? *(correcting himself)* Oh yes, in a week's time. You know I spend half of my time in Lagos and the other half in Port Harcourt.

TONY     You've been here for a week now.

JOHNNY     Time flies when one is happy *(looking at Loretta admiringly)* in love.

TONY     But business is business.

JOHNNY     Indeed! I must divide my time between pleasure and work.

TONY     And in Port Harcourt a lot of work awaits you.

JOHNNY     Yes, indeed! Competition there is becoming more and more fierce.

TONY     Why not concentrate all your business in Lagos?

LORETTA     Oh yes, Johnny, concentrate your business here. I must have you more often with me. Haven't you had enough of living in hotels?

JOHNNY    In hotels?

TONY      When you're in Port Harcourt of course! What's wrong?

JOHNNY    *(realizing his blunder)*. O my head is in the clouds! I've had
          enough, more than enough of hotels. I'm fed up to the teeth.
          Most of them are so shabby.

LORETTA   Most of them overflow with bitches roaming about the corridors
          soliciting customers.

JOHNNY    Tony and I don't go in for that sort of thing.

TONY      One woman, one man.

JOHNNY    Such is our motto.

TONY      O.K. I'll give you a call in a few days.

JOHNNY    Oh yes, if I'm away, Loretta will be around!

LORETTA   I'll be around. Loyal to my post, as a good housewife. Goodbye
          Tony, *(giving him a peck)* I must tidy up things in the kitchen.
          *(carrying the tray with cups and the coffee pot, going towards
          the kitchen)* Ciao Tony! *(she goes out)*

• • •

# ACT III

## SCENE IV

*The Same. John Briggs' sitting room — Lagos*

TONY      *(whispering to Johnny)*. Be careful my dear! Having a double
          life is very good, but you'd better watch what you say. You
          nearly put your foot in your mouth! For goodness' sake be
          careful. As for the briefcase you came with from Port Harcourt,
          give it to me now. I'll take care of it. That will be safer than
          putting it in the paws of a third person. When you go back, I'll

give it back to you and take the other attache case, the one containing all the little things pointing to your new life.

JOHNNY     Oh Tony, how could I ever thank you? To me you are a brother, a father and a mother at the same time. Here, take the briefcase. *(he gives it to him)*

TONY     *(taking the briefcase)*. Bye. I'll see you soon. *(he leaves)*

.   .   .

# ACT III

## SCENE V

*The Same. John Briggs' sitting room — Lagos.*

JOHNNY     *(settling in an armchair, making himself comfortable, apparently self-satisfied)*. A life of luxury, my dear Johnny, that's what awaits you, in this beautiful and luxurious house, with a very lovely mistress, and deluxe too! The only pitfall is the string of disasters which may fall on my head on making the least mistake. *(looking worried)* A wrong move is always possible... *(serene again)* I must keep an eye open for trouble.

LORETTA     *(out of the kitchen rushing towards Johnny)*. Oh Johnny, at last only you and me, how happy I am! *(she cuddles and embraces him)* It's our pre-wedding honeymoon, but our wedding isn't too far away. Right?

JOHNNY     *(pulling a wry face unnoticed by her)*. It won't be long, darling! In a few months we'll be husband and wife.

LORETTA     *(more tenderly)*. In a few months Johnny. That's long. In a few weeks rather I can already see myself wearing a white wedding dress, with a long train.

JOHNNY     *(grimacing)*. And me in a dress suit with a top hat.

LORETTA   Johnny, don't go to Port Harcourt. Don't leave me alone. A week's honeymoon is too short Johnny.

JOHNNY    But Lori I must attend to my business. I can't give up everything, can I?

LORETTA   Then take me to Port Harcourt.

JOHNNY    I wish I could, but it's simply impossible. I have to work from early morning till late in the evening, and, sometimes, even at night. Starting very early in the morning. By 6.30 a.m. I must already be in the arena.

LORETTA   I don't care. I shall patiently wait for you at the hotel. Like the sweet little wife I hope to make.

JOHNNY    Impossible! Your presence will harm my business. When I work I need all my attention and all my energy! Business is difficult you know with competition being unbelievably aggressive.

LORETTA   It's that bad?

JOHNNY    It is! What's more my darling, I must earn a sizeable income. How else could I give you the lifestyle you deserve? Now, there being two of us, I have to work twice as hard.

LORETTA   *(half-believing).* You sound right. But oh, to be separated from you half of the time!

JOHNNY    What about me Lori? You think I'll be happy deep down in my heart to be away from you for so long, while we're in the middle of our honeymoon. Believe me, business is business and there's little we can do about it. All the same, you'll love me the more when I'm back, and I'll love you the more too. That will be some compensation, won't it?

LORETTA   What of your love affairs?

JOHNNY    I have only one love, you. You're not to worry, darling.

LORETTA   You'll telephone me daily, won't you?

JOHNNY    *(seeing the danger).* You know the telephone works only when it wishes, so don't be too demanding. Lori, you can't imagine how much I adore you.

LORETTA    And I'm burning all over ... head to toe. Johnny, it's permanent fire I have inside me. None can put it out except you.

JOHNNY    Lori, you take me unawares, but I'll by and by concentrate my business in Lagos so as to spend less and less time in Port Harcourt.

LORETTA    *(throwing herself into his arms)*. Oh, Johnny I'm so happy you're so nice an angel you know! *(amorously)* come ... come Johnny, let's make the most of the few days left to conjugate the verb 'to love' ... come my angel *(kissing him)* come!

JOHNNY    *(murmuring to himself)*. An angel, as well as a specialist in putting out fires. *(aloud)* I'm all yours my darling, all yours.

*(the curtain falls)*

# ACT IV

## SCENE 1

*John Briggs' sitting-room in Port Harcourt.*

*A man passes carrying a signboard on which is written in capital letters:*
*PORT HARCOURT, JANUARY 20.*

JOHNNY   *(alone)* At last in Port Harcourt!  What peace after those two
         wild weeks in Lagos. Peace that is welcome but which would
         soon bore me to death. Human nature is really paradoxical.
         Man is never satisfied with what he has. But poor me, besides
         this universal failing which affects me, I suffer from fits of
         middle-age lust! In the end, time may take care of everything,
         but in the meanwhile there's so much to account for. *(pointing
         at his suitcase)*  I have a hoard of beautiful things in there
         which I'll bring out when my wife is around. *(sitting on an
         armchair)*  How sweet it is to have two homes, finding in one
         what's not to be found in the other! Here, it's a fruit juice and
         lemonade diet. In the other, over there in Lagos, a whisky and
         champagne cure. Isn't that great? One allowing me to recover
         from the excesses of the other. The other to relieve me from the
         inherent boredom of the first. *(laughing)* What exceptional
         living! So many will be plainly envious! That's plain enough.

· · ·

# ACT IV

## SCENE II

*John Briggs' sitting-room in Port Harcourt.*

ANGELA     *(from the door).* Oh, you're here already!

JOHNNY     Already. See how anxious I am, to see you and the kids. How bored can one be in mighty Lagos that people claim to find so lively! New year's day was particularly dull. Most of my time I spent in my hotel-room reading and sleeping, and having a frugal meal.

ANGELA     Oh, my poor darling! You'd surely have appreciated the meal I prepared.

JOHNNY     Well, business is business.

ANGELA     On such a day?

JOHNNY     One must earn one's bread and butter. It's in Lagos I am earning it. And well, the more we are the more it costs.

ANGELA     Is that a reproach? Are you becoming stingy in your old age?

JOHNNY     Stingy me? Am I an old fogey already?

ANGELA     Well, you're no longer in the first flush of youth.

JOHNNY     What horrible things can assail the ears of a man sacrificing himself for his family! Even on the New Year Day I was bored to death in a hotel room, instead of being with my family around a table, to savour the exquisite dishes prepared by my dear wife. And what encomiums fall to my lot!

ANGELA     Come Johnny. Don't make such a fuss. I said it all jokingly.

JOHNNY     Okay darling, all is forgiven. come and see all the good and beautiful things I've brought for you from Lagos.

ANGELA     Where?

JOHNNY     In my suitcase. *(going towards the suitcase)* Wait a minute! Let me open it.

ANGELA      *(getting near the case)* Hurry up! I'm impatient to see all those things!

JOHNNY      *(opening it gently).* The Pandora's box or the chest of wonders?

ANGELA      The chest of wonders.

JOHNNY      *(bringing a dress out of the case).* Here's for Madam!

ANGELA      Oh how beautiful! I love the colours and the design. *(kissing Johnny)* You're a darling!

JOHNNY      *(bringing out toys and books)* And for the children! A second father Christmas, that's what I am.

ANGELA      How happy they'll be when they come back this evening!

JOHNNY      I'll be happy just seeing them. And now the choice piece of this miraculous catch! *(bringing a small parcel out of the case)* This, darling, is for you!

ANGELA      *(who grabs it eagerly).* Oh Johnny, what's it? *(untying the ribbon around the parcel and tearing in her haste the wrapping paper)* What's it Johnny? What's it?

JOHNNY      Be patient darling!

ANGELA      Be patient, be patient, *(finally discovering what the parcel contains).* Oh Johnny! *(bringing out a necklace and gazing at it)* How beautiful! *(kissing him)* You are the best of all husbands! *(continuing to admire it)* It's beautiful!

JOHNNY      *(brings out the large-sized photograph of a woman from the suitcase) (murmuring to himself).* But, what's that? Loretta in a boubou!

ANGELA      What are you looking at?

JOHNNY      *(suddenly in cold sweat).* Nothing. A document that mistakenly slipped in here?

ANGELA      Let me see it.

JOHNNY      *(hiding it behind his back).* For nothing in the world would I mix presents with business documents! Look, you better go and admire yourself in the mirror in your room. This necklace fits you perfectly. Really, I made a lucky choice.

ANGELA    You're right. I'll go and see myself in the mirror. *(she leaves, still admiring the necklace)*

JOHNNY    *(putting the photograph back in the suitcase, and mopping his brow).* Phew, I got a real fright! But who could have put that photograph in my case if not Loretta herself. That's her all right! Let's see what's left in the suitcase. *(he searches it meticulously, inspecting one by one, all the things left)* I wouldn't be surprised to find other things implicating me. *(discovering a photograph of Loretta in bikini)* Here's another picture of her in bikini this time. Upon my word, this suitcase is almost a bran tub. Oh Loretta, my divine love! You'd like to cover the walls of my hotel room with souvenirs of yourself. That's just like you. *(running towards the book case)* Let's hide these photographs, quickly, we'll dispose of them later. *(continuing his search, extracting Loretta's bras and panties)* Loretta, Loretta, for God's sake, these are things you shouldn't do to a poor family man like me who is entering his purgatory on earth! *(shoving them in his pocket as fast as he can)* Let's hide these quickly to avoid storm, lightning, thunder! She did all that with the best of intentions. From now on I'll be more vigilant. Neither wife nor mistress must surreptitiously slip into my case or any of my pockets a compromising object. Let's grin and bear it for now. Double life is subject to the same surprises as anything else. One must pass through a period of apprenticeship or initiation! Not everybody is a born rogue! Ah, I hear my wife approaching. Be careful my dear Johnny. Be careful with your words and your acts. Don't forget you're just an apprentice in this very entertaining way of life, but oh, how treacherous!

. . .

# ACT IV

## SCENE III

*John Briggs' house in Port Harcourt.*

ANGELA   It's really beautiful! Its splendour goes very well with my white dress. Oh Johnny! *(kissing him)* You're so adorable! So nice! So sweet! You're indeed the best of husbands!

JOHNNY   *(who has been counting the number of compliments on his fingers) (aside)* Four, five, not so bad. *(aloud)* And you the most affectionate, and understanding of wives. So sweet! Such a darling! A jewel! Beside, the best of mothers.

ANGELA   *(who has also been counting on her fingers) (aside)*. Six! One more than me! He has surpassed himself! That's good. There's improvement in his compliments. *(aloud)* Johnny, I love you. But I undergo terrible ordeals being separated from you. Why can't I come to Lagos to stay with you? I'm not scared of living in a hotel.

JOHNNY   Angela darling, I'd love it, but it's impossible. I work from early morning till late in the evening and sometimes even at night! And you know, at 6.00 a.m., I'm already on my way to work, to avoid the terrible Lagos traffic jams!

ANGELA   I don't care! I'll wait patiently for you in the hotel-room like the good dear wife that I am.

JOHNNY   *(who turns his back on her and makes expressive grimaces).* Believe me Angela, the more I think, the more I realize it's impossible. Your presence would affect business. When I work I must retain the use of all my faculties and I need all my energy. *(aside)* I'm giving word for word all the sweet talk I dished up for Loretta. I've acquired a taste for love affairs and deceit! *(to Angela)* Business is hard you know and the competition is incredibly aggressive.

ANGELA   Is it that bad? Really!

JOHNNY   Could be worse in fact. The more we are the harder it is to make a living. To be able to offer you the lifestyle you are used to, I must slave away twice as hard. I'm afraid that from now on, every month, I may have to spend three complete weeks in Lagos.

ANGELA     Three weeks! Without being back at the weekends? That's dreadful! Johnny ...

JOHNNY     *(interrupting).* It's even more dreadful for me. Is it my wish that I should be three weeks, twenty-one long days, far from you and the kids! Business is business!

ANGELA     What about your family life? Does it not matter to you?

JOHNNY     I'm doing my best Angela ...

ANGELA     We'll have to find a way out together.

JOHNNY     *(worried).* A way out?

ANGELA     We can all move to Lagos? If you are destined to spend the greatest part of your time in Lagos, then let's live in Lagos, you, I and the children.

JOHNNY     *(not knowing what to say).* Oh, you know life in Lagos is not all rosy. It's far from being a paradise! *(the door bell rings)* Who can that be?

o ● o

# ACT IV

## SCENE IV

*The same.*

ANGELA     *(moving towards the door).* No idea! *(opening it for the visitor)* Ah, it's you Tony! Please come in. Yes, Johnny is here. *(embracing Tony)* You're welcome.

TONY        *(moving towards Johnny)*. Old pal, how are you? How did you celebrate your New Year eve and the New Year day?

JOHNNY      I was in Lagos my dear. You can scarcely imagine how bored I was! I stayed in the hotel to read and sleep, having only a frugal meal. The next day which was a Sunday I attended the high mass at the cathedral. There was a very good choir you know. It's the best moment I had, with the reading of a chapter from the old testament.

TONY        *(aside)*. You old devil! You're already a master in the art of lying and pretence. *(aloud)* Those are sound activities, I must say, especially for starting the new year.

ANGELA      Johnny, you know, is a very good Christian. Practising regularly. He wouldn't miss a Mass.

TONY        *(aside)*. Let him specify which kind of practice and what kind of mass. There is mass, and mass. Each has not the same colour! *(aloud)* Johnny is surely among those who follow the straight and narrow path!

ANGELA      A path which could hardly be straighter!

TONY        True! *(aside)* My dear if only you knew the other face of your star of a husband!

JOHNNY      Come on now, don't exaggerate! I do from time to time, like everybody else, make a few detours from the straight and narrow path.

ANGELA      Maybe, but they are minor detours.

TONY        Yes, a few meanders like those of a river trying hard to reach the sea.

JOHNNY      Life's indeed a river which flows from birth to death.

TONY        From nothing to nothing.

ANGELA      Ungodly fellow! Miscreant! Tony! How could you say such shocking thing? It's from paradise to paradise that life flows. Of course it could be from paradise to hell.

| TONY | Excuse me Angela. Sometimes I have my doubts. The water at times is very low and muddy and then it cannot flow from anything to anything. |
|---|---|
| JOHNNY | Life is a river, which sometimes flows rapidly like a torrent, at other times slowly, lazily, and taking maybe ages to reach the sea! |
| ANGELA | O.K. Enough of philosophy! Tony I will make you an arbiter in a discussion which we had just started when you arrived. |
| JOHNNY | Moving to Lagos? |
| ANGELA | That's it! |
| JOHNNY | *(making conspiratorial gestures in the back of Angela)* Well, I'm sure Tony will share the same views. Put him in the picture about your projects, and you'll see what he thinks. I won't intervene in your discussion, not wanting to influence him. |
| ANGELA | I'm grateful. Look, Tony, Johnny is talking of spending three weeks a month in Lagos instead of two without even coming back at weekends. I suggested that we all move to Lagos thus have our home in Lagos itself! |
| TONY | Angela, my very Angela, I must interrupt you immediately! Your idea is impracticable! First of all, the rents are exorbitant in Lagos, ten times as high as at Port Harcourt. What's more, vacant houses are rare! As for buying an apartment, let's not even talk about it. That would cost you millions of naira. What's more, insecurity is rampant! Thefts with house breakings are a daily affair and armed robberies common occurrences day and night. |
| ANGELA | *(her face marked with apprehension)* Seriously, Tony, is that Lagos? |
| TONY | That's Lagos all right, Angela dear! I'm not exaggerating, nor adding an iota. And the accidents, Angela! My God! Just thinking of the dangers your children are courting while going to school and coming back would get on your nerves. Poor kids! I won't mention the go-slow. But the terrible traffic jams |

can turn a pleasant ride into a nightmare. Once, it took me six hours to go from Apapa to Ikoyi.

ANGELA    Six hours! From Apapa to Ikoyi? But that's crazy! Insane! *(almost in tears)* How can anyone live under such conditions?

TONY    One adjusts somehow. You have to manage you know. Believe me. Angela, it's mere survival there rather than living.

ANGELA    That's awful!

TONY    That word isn't strong enough. You can raise your hat to Johnny who accepts such conditions of ... of survival, being obliged to increase his monthly stay in Lagos to three weeks. But your husband is a hero, my dear Angela, who should be decorated with a medal of the OSF!

ANGELA    OSF?

TONY    Yes, OSF! Order of the Sacrifice to the Family — if such Order existed!

JOHNNY    Tony, permit me to put my oar in. It's with a sense of painful regret that I shall have to spend an extra week in the big hole called Lagos. When I could have been so cosy with my family, in a warm atmosphere and a complete peace of mind. I've had enough of it, Tony. I've had more than I can take of Lagos. O my children! Whom I'll have on my knees for just a week in a month instead of two. But I accept all this because of the well-being of my family! One must always face up to difficulties. The family must come first, always.

TONY    *(interrupting him)* Business is business!

ANGELA    I see we're not going to move to Lagos. I'll have to put up with my hard fate.

TONY    And Johnny to put up with his own.

JOHNNY    *(pretending to be sad).* The hard fate of a husband and father in exile!

ANGELA    I've been talking, and forgetting my duties as a hostess! Tony, can I offer you something? A cup of coffee?

TONY  With pleasure, ma' am.

ANGELA  Johnny of course will have coffee. I'll be right back. *(she goes out)*

● ● ●

# ACT IV

## SCENE V
*The same.*

JOHNNY  My dear Tony, you've played your role magnificently! She's not going to talk about moving to Lagos for a long time.

TONY  You got a real fright my dear! I came at the right time, or she would have been ready to pack up and go to Lagos in the shortest time possible.

JOHNNY  It's Loretta who would have had to pull up a long face.

TONY  True! But Loretta is Loretta and Angela is Angela your wife.

JOHNNY  It's not easy to live a double life. To climb up to paradise, one may have to get seared by the fires of hell!

TONY  My dear Johnny, on this good earth nothing comes easy. But you're sure of never getting bored with such a life.

JOHNNY  Certainly not! I hope so.

TONY  It is boredom you were mostly complaining about?

JOHNNY  Certainly! Sandwiched between the two ladies I no longer risk being bored.

TONY  Sandwiched ... *(he starts laughing)*. Like a slice of ham between two slices of bread.

JOHNNY  I wonder if one day I would not be flattened, crushed by one of them!

TONY       You need have no fears. You're the one calling the tune. They
           won't know what's going on. You'll be able to continue playing
           this delicious comedy as long as you wish, so long as you don't
           make stupid mistakes.

JOHNNY     That's true. I derive immense pleasure from this love affair. I
           have the feeling of being a violinist virtuoso running his bow
           on two violins at the same time.

TONY       That's a nice way to express yourself, Mister dramatist,
           comedian, producer of your masterpiece which I may call *the
           paradise of Johnny Briggs!* But we'd better shut up. Angela
           should soon come back.

JOHNNY     How lucky that spoken words fly off and don't stay on like the
           written ones! *Verba volant, scripta manent,* they say! *(lowering
           his voice).* Let's be quiet. Here's Angela.

TONY       *(whispering to Johnny).* I'll be as silent as the grave on that
           topic. *(aloud on seeing Angela entering).* I can perceive from
           here the exquisite aroma of the coffee you're bringing, Angela.

ANGELA     *(coming near them).* Here's your nectar quite hot almost boiling!

JOHNNY     Thanks indeed! Am I not the luckiest of men?

TONY       He never stops praising you.

ANGELA     *(who pours the coffee in the cups, a smile on her lips).* Very
           flattered! You're both very nice. I'm lucky to have such a
           husband and such a friend!

TONY       *(savouring his coffee in small sips).* And how happy am I to
           have friends like the two of you!

JOHNNY     *(doing the same).* Friendship is a priceless precious stone!

ANGELA     It's worth more than the most beautiful of gems.

TONY       Without friends man is like an orphan on earth. *(putting his
           cup on the table).* Well, Angela, I could do with another cup.
           Your coffee is real first-class!

ANGELA    *(serving him another cup).* Your wish is my command.

TONY    Johnny, when're you going back to Lagos?

JOHNNY    In a week my dear. I have to be there on the 27th. I have an important appointment. The person I've to meet would never accept postponement or delay.

TONY    Business is business. That's the story we have to live with always, we poor knights of the business! We are real slaves to this accursed business, isn't it Johnny?

JOHNNY    Business is business as you say so well!

TONY    Yet come as often as you can to Port Harcourt. Think of the kids who'd love to see their dad more often!

JOHNNY    I promise not to overlook such a possibility.

ANGELA    But by the way, why not give me the telephone number of the hotel where you will lodge?

JOHNNY    *(showing annoyance).* Oh well, I'm never in the same hotel. Always, I've to keep moving from one corner of Lagos to another, and there are more than twenty districts.

ANGELA    More than twenty!

JOHNNY    If you like I can list them for you. *(reciting them in one breath)* Lagos Island, Surulere, Yaba, Ikeja ...

TONY    Agege, Mushin, Ilupeju, Ebute-Metta *(regaining his breath),* Victoria Island, Ikoyi and the rest.

JOHNNY    Somolu, Oshodi, Maryland, Tin Can, Iddo, and I surely forget some!

TONY    And I don't count the little towns situated around Lagos: Shagamu, Epe, Ijebu-Ode...

JOHNNY    Ikorodu, Badagry and so on and so forth!

ANGELA    In fact, more than twenty! But this Lagos is a megalopolis!

TONY    Yes, a Monster of a town which hasn't finished growing.

JOHNNY    So I don't have a fixed place. I roam around Lagos at the mercy of business.

TONY      Business is business!

ANGELA    Yes, indeed. I am always in the dark.

TONY      What do you mean?

ANGELA    In the shadow of my husband I mean, like the shrub under the foliage of a big tree.

TONY      That's a nice image Angela. Upon my word Angela *(smiling)* you make a very charming shrub and him *(pointing at Johnny)* a magnificent tree! Now I must run off. Johnny I'll see you before you leave. By the way, when are you leaving, on the 26th or on the 27th?

JOHNNY    On the 27th. I'll take the first flight. I have all the time. My appointment is at 11.00 a.m.. I wouldn't like to rob Angela of one night.

TONY      That would be an unforgivable offence.

ANGELA    An attack on the rights of the wife.

JOHNNY    A crime against womanhood.

TONY      A crime of *lese feminity*. On these beautiful words, bye bye. Be seeing you, Ciao! *(he goes out)*.

*(the curtain falls)*

# ACT V

## SCENE I

*The same man passes carrying his signboard*
*indicating LAGOS, FEBRUARY 10.*

LORETTA   *(in a mocking tone)*. Johnny, you dreamt again last night.
Among the words I managed to catch, the word 'Angel' or
something like that kept coming back. Your mumblings were
not distinct but they gave the feeling that you were talking to
someone.

JOHNNY   *(worried)*. You know Lori, in dreams one can say anything.
The mumblings that issue out of someone's lips arc often only
cock and bull stories.

LORETTA   Johnny, in your dreams you were communicating with angels
and heaven, it seems to me.

JOHNNY   *(Reassured)*. I never remember my dreams.

LORETTA   I am sure because you spoke the word angel ten times in two
minutes.

JOHNNY   Ten times, Lori?

LORETTA   Yes indeed. You must have been in deep conversation with
those blessed creatures!

• • •

# ACT V

## SCENE II

*The man carrying his signboard comes in running, as Loretta goes out.*
*One can read on the signboard: PORT HARCOURT, FEBRUARY 18*

ANGELA   *(who comes in while the man goes out)*. Johnny, you dreamt
again last night. Among the words which came out of your

mouth, I think I heard something like 'Lorry' coming up again
and again. These mumblings were not very audible. But they
gave the feeling that you were invoking someone or something.

JOHNNY     *(worried).* Is that so? Listen to me, Angela. You're not going
to attach any importance to a dream, are you? One could say
the worst trash in a dream. No wonder, the mumblings which
issue out of a dreamer's mouth are often incoherent and
senseless.

ANGELA     Well, I have my own idea about that. When you were repeating
Lorrie, Lorrie, you were invoking business affairs of yours I
guess!

JOHNNY     *(reassured).* Well, being in the motor-vehicles business, the
lorries must come one's way. In fact, they are a major part of
my turnover.

ANGELA     When someone repeats the word 'Lorrie' ten times in two
minutes ...

JOHNNY     Ten times! In two minutes?

ANGELA     This shows that your mind must be completely taken over by
your business of Lorries in Lagos.

JOHNNY     *(feigning surprise).* Ten times? In two minutes!

• • •

# ACT V

## SCENE III

*The man reappears with his signboard, while Angela goes out of the
room. One can read: LAGOS, MARCH 20*

*The man leaves the moment Loretta appears.*

LORETTA    Johnny, how's your business in Port Harcourt? As engrossing
as ever?

JOHNNY    More than ever, darling. In Port Harcourt there's a boom. The black gold is flowing freely.

*(The man reappears running while the signboard indicates: LAGOS, APRIL 1ST. And Loretta disappears as fast as she can. Angela appears, sees the signboard indicating Lagos, goes out and then comes back undecided)*

THE MAN    *(to himself).* Fools' day! I was only joking. Today is the 1st of April. *(turning the signboard).* It's Port Harcourt you should read!

ANGELA    *(coming back while the man is going).* So Johnny, how is your business in Lagos? Still as flourishing?

JOHNNY    More than ever my darling. In Lagos there's a boom. Money is flowing freely! *(the man appears again and Angela leaves. He starts a ballet with a fast rhythm in which the man appears five consecutive times. His signboard shows a different date and place each time. Loretta and Angela appear and disappear turn by turn, while Johnny is motionless like a statue not saying a single word. The five appearances can be prolonged or cut short at the discretion of the director). (NOTE: The two ladies could be motionless, one sitting on the left, one on the right and Johnny moving fast from one to the other).*

• • •

# ACT V

## SCENE IV

*The man, who has regained a normal rhythm, appears with his signboard showing LAGOS, JULY 10, while Angela goes away.*

TONY    *(who comes in behind Johnny while the man with the signboard goes away).* So Loretta is not here.

JOHNNY    She went to see her mother. But my dear Tony I have
          something to tell you.

TONY      I'm listening.

JOHNNY    Well, I've had enough!

TONY      Enough of what?

JOHNNY    Enough of a double life! I am unable to play the two parts. I
          make so many blunders that I'm within a hair's breath of
          catastrophe several times a day! I can no longer sleep, my dear
          Tony. What is worse, I mumble in my dreams.

TONY      At night? In the hearing of your bed-mate? But they do not
          understand, do they?

JOHNNY    But they might one day. When in Port Harcourt I dream of
          Loretta, and when in Lagos I dream of Angela! And the last
          straw, to crown it all, is that I shout their names in my dreams!

TONY      Their names? They should be mad then.

JOHNNY    They will be, it seems.

TONY      Do you cry their names out of love?

JOHNNY    Out of infatuation or maybe fear. I don't know!

TONY      My dear Johnny, by loving two women at the same time
          you're accomplishing a miracle.

JOHNNY    My heart may be large enough to accommodate two loves, but
          my brain is certainly too small!

TONY      So?

JOHNNY    I've had enough my dear Tony. More than enough! I am fed
          up! I really feel like sending them all packing, wife, children,
          mistress to become a Buddhist monk meditating in the Hima-
          layas!

TONY      *(bursts out laughing)*. A Buddhist monk? In the Himalayas?
          You, John Briggs? You know the Himalayas are ice-cold, and
          I can't see you, Johnny Briggs, spinning your prayer wheel in

the blizzards!

JOHNNY    You may laugh till you can laugh no more. But I am sick of it all!

TONY    Why, why, why? You've led a blissful double life for more than six months and you've never been caught!

JOHNNY    Living like that with a Sword of Damocles suspended over one's head, the stress is too great!

TONY    Come on Johnny, exercise patience! Do you wish to break up with Loretta, such a nice and pretty face?

JOHNNY    Far from it!

TONY    Or you wish to repudiate Angela, the mother of your children, yet as beautiful as ever?

JOHNNY    I love her, I love her, I love her!

TONY    So?

JOHNNY    I am caught in a trap! And there's no way out.

TONY    Things will sort themselves out, believe me!

JOHNNY    I wish they would, I wish they would. But in the meantime ...

TONY    In the meantime, let's not give up in haste. Himalayas would require even more of patience.

JOHNNY    Believe me, I believe you.

TONY    *(laughing)*. I've no complaints on that score.

JOHNNY    *(laughing)*. Oh, you're an expert at raising a laugh! *(they disappear)*.

• • •

# ACT V

## SCENE V

*The man with the signboard walks in slowly. One can read on the signboard: LAGOS, SEPTEMBER 20. Johnny briggs then reappears while the man leaves slowly.*

JOHNNY    *(shattered, looking at his empty hands).* My briefcase! My briefcase! How could I forget my briefcase in a taxi? I must be really stupid or absent-minded to do such a thing! To forget my briefcase with Loretta's pictures and letters inside! You should see the letter, so passionate, so fiery! What about the address book, in which my Ikoyi address is clearly written as well as those of my girlfriends whom I visit from time to time to take my mind off things and give myself an extra good time! What a scatterbrain you are my poor chap! You'll have to go far to find such an imbecile! This forgetfulness may cost you your paradise and even your purgatory! My cheque-book, my driver's licence, the one thousand naira and the five hundred dollars, all gone, and Loretta's love letters and photographs, some in scanty dresses, also gone *(he paces back and forth, very excited).* A shot of whisky may do me some good *(pouring himself a large shot).* And put me back in my senses! *(drinking half the glass).* But why am I over-taxing myself so much? What will the taxi driver do on finding a briefcase? Certainly not return it to the owner! He will open it, take whatever seems valuable, and fling away the rest! By now Loretta's letters may be flowing somewhere in a Mushin gutter or elsewhere and her pictures may be pinned up in a bachelor's shack in Ajegunle. But I remember now! I wasn't alone in the taxi! There was an honourable-looking old man with me. He must have realized that I forgot something. What would he do! Give it to the driver? Take it to the police station? Or simply keep it for himself? Anyhow, I don't know the gentleman, so he is not in a position to return the briefcase to me. *(thoughtfully).* At a certain moment he stared at me as if he knew me! Come on, keep quiet, he must have mistaken me for somebody else! Anyhow whatever happens, let it happen! *(he goes out).*

# ACT V

## SCENE VI

*The man with the signboard comes in showing: PORT HARCOURT, SEPTEMBER 22.*

ANGELA *(who enters holding a briefcase while the man goes out) (talking to someone outside).* Once again, thank you Sir. It's very nice of you to have brought my husband's briefcase from Lagos up to here. He will thank you himself when he comes back, goodbye! *(closing the door and putting the attache case on the floor).* But this attache case is different from the one he uses! Nevertheless, it's his. His name is written in big letters on the label stuck on it; JOHN BRIGGS. There's no mistake possible, although there's no address! Maybe the other one has a faulty lock, or some other flaw. *(turning around the attache case)* I must say that it excites my curiosity in the highest degree. What's in it? I would give a lot to know. But how do I know without opening it? Let's see whether it's locked! *(trying to open it).* It is as I suspected! What shall I do? An inner force is pushing me to open it, while my conscience forbids me to do it! *(continuing to turn it around)* That's just too bad. Come what may, I'll open the case. It's a lock with a combination. With a bit of luck I'll succeed without having to force it open. *(trying several numbers without success)* If I don't succeed in the next five minutes I'll use brutal force! *(Continuing to fiddle around with the lock)* Ah, I have unbelievable luck! *(opening the attache case)* I have opened it, I have opened it *(shouting joyfully),* I have opened it! Almost without any effort! *(looking at the open attache case)* Now, let's see what John Briggs' number two briefcase contains! *(first searching the pockets)* One thousand naira in ten naira notes. Well, well, dollars! I ought to count them. It's hard foreign currency. *(counting them)* Five hundred exactly. A cheque-book, a driving licence, a calculator. O.K. Now let's see the main part. Fancy the photographs! Let's see these! *(taking a picture and looking at it)* But it's him, John Briggs, my dear husband, cuddling a young girl very tenderly! *(looking at another one)*

Here's the same young person in bikini! And there is something written at the back. What! 'To Johnny forever!' And she signs Loretta. Well, what a mess! *(looking at the other pictures)* And they are all of the same sort! Well, well, my bastard of a husband isn't doing badly at all! And these pictures were taken in a luxurious house, having all the comforts! Wouldn't it by any chance be the kind of hotel my dear husband frequents? Well, well, just fancy that. Tony is there also, cuddling another young woman, good looking too upon my word! *(Bringing out a pack of letters tied up with a pink ribbon and taking a sniff at them)* Letters, what's more, perfumed. These are Loretta's letters, this harlot, that's for sure! And he carries them in his attache case because he can't carry them on his heart. Bastard! Dirty pig! I'll read one or two just to see the style, that will be enough for me. I'm sure they'll be full of the same rubbish! *(taking a letter from the pack and reading it)* Yes, it's just what I expected ... rubbish ... absolute rubbish. Words of love which would make one want to cry with laughter more than anything else! Let's see the other one. Well, well, it's more serious ... they're talking about marriage. Well, can you imagine? My husband has made a promise of marriage to this tart! *(moving towards the phone)* Well, I have to tell mother first about this discovery! She'll have a good laugh! *(dialling the number and speaking to her mother)* Is that you mother? How are you? Fine? Well, so much the better! Why so much the better? Because you're going to be sorely disappointed! In fact, disgusted! So hold on tight to a piece of furniture. Better still, get a chair and sit down. *(with a sob)* Mother I've been deceived! Grossly deceived! Grossly deceived! Johnny is deceiving me and shamefully too! ... Yes, mother he has been terribly unfaithful to me ... Since when? I don't know. I can't say! *(the sobs increases)* ... Do you think that the bastard keeps me informed about his sleeping around! ... No, don't come, I'll call you when I know more about it. Thanks, my dear mum! ... Oh you need it, you know! ... Middle-age lust? ... Oh, that's what this illness is called!... Well, I'll play the doctor and I'll cure the bastard quickly of his illness. ... A dirty pig! That's what he is. Goodbye mother, lots of kisses! *(hanging up)* And now let's continue our search! Oh here's the main piece of the puzzle, a prime piece, his address book. Let's see! I'm sure that all this is grist to my mill. First let's see the letter L., I suspected as much! First on the list, Loretta Effiong. A Calabar girl I am sure. I can see from the name ... From what people say, these Efik or Ibibio girls make up the largest group of prostitutes operating in Lagos. Address: 1201 Bourdillon Road Ikoyi, Telephone 50.401 OK!

Now to the letter B. Well there's no name but two initials, J.B. Address: 1201 Bourdillon Road Ikoyi, Telephone 50.401! No doubts, it's John Briggs, my dear husband! So they're living under the same roof and what's more in Ikoyi, in the most exclusive area of Lagos! He does not over-tax himself, my dear husband, living together with a high standard prostitute in a luxury apartment! When I think again of all the stories he has told me, his sad and boring life in Lagos, with traffic jams and insecurity, going from one hotel to another depending on his business. Trust a man and see what you've got coming to you. A man in whom I had complete confidence and who I raised to the skies! Well, well, lower down there's another address without either name or initials this time. But with a telephone number. Broad Street, Lagos Island, telephone number 55.421. It's probably the address of his office ... anyway it's easy to verify, I only have to telephone!

And that pig never told me he had an office! The hidden face of this man is really very vast, it's incredible! Let's try that number. *(dialling the number)* zero-one-five-five-four-two-one. It's ringing engaged! Let's try again ... engaged! *(trying ten times)* Engaged! Engaged! O NITEL! You drive me crazy! It's ringing this time, great! Hello! Lagos! five-five-four-two-one? Could I speak to Mr. Briggs please ... yes Mr. Briggs, John Briggs ... yes, his wife speaking. Yes, his wife. No it's not a joke! Oh you didn't know he was married. Well he is, madam. To me who is speaking to you! I'll wait, madam. *(nervous)* But what the hell is this silly girl doing! *(looking at her watch)* Oh, at last! What! He had to leave urgently for London! Let me laugh! I repeat: let me laugh. Well, then tell him when he comes back that he can go to China, to Kamtchatka or to the moon ... *(shouting)* Yes, to the moon! *(hanging up violently)* The moon!

**(*The curtain falls*)**

# ACT VI

## SCENE I

*Angela goes out while the man enters with his signboard showing:
LAGOS, SEPTEMBER 26.*

JOHNNY      *(aside)* That's it, she has found out what has been going on. Now she has all the addresses, and she'll show up at **Bourdillon** Road at any time from now!

LORETTA      *(furious, showing him the letter she is holding)*. Well my dear, well done your claiming to be a bachelor! A wife and six children! A fourty-five year old bachelor who promised to marry me, who took me as a virgin and to whom I gave my innocence, my body, my heart. *(in tears)* Yes, my heart, with all my heart.

JOHNNY      *(taking the letter and recognizing his wife's writing)*. **Virgin!** Stop exaggerating! You lost that treasure donkey's years ago. *(aside)* The bitch didn't waste time! As soon as she laid hands on the address book she found my address and wrote to **Loretta** by speed-post! I would not be surprised if she shows up on the first plane! *(to Loretta)* Darling, when did you receive that letter?

LORETTA      Darling, you said! You, who have cheated me shamelessly for months! You who told me while going to Port Harcourt that business is business!

JOHNNY      Come on, my darling!

LORETTA      Shut up! Don't say that word again in my presence! There's no more darling, there's only a woman deceived, exploited, shamelessly held up to ridicule. You don't know what you expose yourself to, ignoring the length to which the vengeance of such a deceived woman can go!

JOHNNY      But I love you Loretta ... *(moving towards her)* I ...

LORETTA     *(who takes two steps backwards).* Don't come near me!

JOHNNY      I'm madly in love with you! You're the only woman who counts for me and I'm ready to leave everything for you!

LORETTA     Me? The only woman who counts for you? How can somebody trust a man who can dump a wife and six children without any remorse?

JOHNNY      Love knows no limitations, my love.

LORETTA     Don't speak that word again!

JOHNNY      *(who comes towards her again).* My heart burns for you.

LORETTA     Your heart? You don't have one. What burns for me is placed much lower on your person.

JOHNNY      Loretta, what does the nasty letter say?

LORETTA     Threats from your wife. If you want to know.

JOHNNY      Don't worry! She'll calm down.

LORETTA     In her shoes I'd have written the same words.

JOHNNY      Oh, you women always dramatize things!

LORETTA     Dramatize? You'll see if I dramatize or if she does. It will be very easy for me to make an ally of the enemy when we come face to face.

JOHNNY      Is she coming?

LORETTA     She is, but I've no fear. Here I'm in my house, and I may refuse to let her enter.

JOHNNY      Your house?

LORETTA     This house was bought in my name, wasn't it?

JOHNNY      It was bought in your name by force of circumstance. I could not buy it in my name without attracting my wife's attention! But now, things being what they are, we shall put things in order. I am the legitimate owner.

LORETTA  Legitimate owner. Oh, the wicked gentleman, who, after having deceived two innocent and trusting ladies, is out to reduce one to poverty! *(becoming very distant)* Well, sir, you should know that this house is mine and that it will remain mine.

JOHNNY  *(trembling with rage)*. We shall soon see who will have the last word!

LORETTA  So much hatred, such rage in your eyes!

JOHNNY  Bitch!

LORETTA  *(haughtily)*. What tender love words you're shouting at me, Sir!

JOHNNY  Slut, hooker, go back where you came from!

LORETTA  If you don't stop, Sir, I'll be forced to dismiss you and ask you to pack up and clear off!

JOHNNY  You have the guts to ask me to leave my own house?

LORETTA  *(mockingly)* Your honour is building castles in the air from what I can see.

JOHNNY  *(pulling at his hair)*. What on earth have I done to be reduced to that?

LORETTA  *(in a more informal tone)*. You thought you were very clever my poor chap! He who grasps at too much loses everything. 'He who sows the wind shall reap the whirlwind'. Beware the man who crosses swords with us! You'll pay for your insults.

. . .

# ACT VI

## SCENE II

*John Briggs' sitting room in Lagos. All John's luggage including a giant trunk are piled up in the centre of the room. Johnny is seated on the floor, alongside the luggage, looking shattered.*

JOHNNY    When I think she refuses me a chair! While this very chair and all the furniture in this room belong to me. Now here I am, homeless like a tramp. At least in Lagos. Now I'm left to see what kind of welcome I'll get at Port Harcourt, provided that Gorgon doesn't arrive here before I leave. Is it wise to pack up and go like a refugee, without being sure whether one would be welcomed or not?

LORETTA   *(coming out of her room).* You're still here?

JOHNNY    Where do you want me to go?

LORETTA   Hotels abound in Lagos and in Apapa, Surulere, Yaba, Ikoyi, and I don't count the little towns around Lagos, Ijebu-Ode, Epe, Badagry, Ikorodu and so many others!

JOHNNY    So you have no pity?

LORETTA   You had none on me!

JOHNNY    And if I decide to stay on as a squatter?

LORETTA   The police is there to help, don't forget. I give you up till tomorrow to clear off. You see I'm magnanimous.

JOHNNY    Magnanimous, indeed!

LORETTA   I've seen enough of you. I'm going back to my work! *(she goes to her room)*

JOHNNY    There's for me no haven of peace where I may drop anchor. Persona non grata from West to East. That's what I've become!

ANGELA    *(who arrives rushing through the main door).* I entered this way, without ringing or knocking, wanting to catch the bird in his nest! *(glancing round the room)* But where on earth is this buffoon, so that I can bash him up? *(turning around and seeing the heap of piled up luggage)* That's his luggage. I recognize one of his suitcases. Is he intending to migrate? It seems to me that I've come right on time.

JOHNNY    *(who tries to hide himself behind the trunk).* What can I expect if not blows raining on my limbs. Ouch! ouch!! ouch!!! I had better number them when they come.

ANGELA     *(running around the stack of baggage without seeing Johnny who is turning around too).* If I ever catch him, hell is going to break loose. He will get the thrashing of his life!

JOHNNY     *(who turning around the heap of luggage trips on a suitcase and falls face-flat at his wife's feet).* I'm dying, I'm dead!

ANGELA:    Well, I have caught you at last my dear little husband! You bird of ill-omen who was getting ready to fly away. *(placing a foot on his stomach)* Well, now let's fight it out! *(the curtain falls briefly and goes up again)*

• • •

# ACT VI

## SCENE III

*The three of them wear obvious signs of a brawl, especially Johnny who has a black eye, with stitches on his face.*

ANGELA     Now I understand the situation much better. My dear Loretta, I'm sorry for having been so rash.

LORETTA    I have been as rash and brutal. Forgive me.

Angela     All through the fault of that monster. We were too confiding and too affectionate.

LORETTA    How true!

ANGELA     *(staring severely at Johnny who is looking contrite and downcast)* But the monster is in a bad way.

LORETTA    He's no longer as proud and flamboyant.

ANGELA     He has lost his arrogance.

LORETTA    He would come and eat from our hands.

ANGELA     We shall decide his fate in camera.

LORETTA    Let's strike while the iron is hot.

ANGELA      And let's also strike this ass, this donkey, whether he's hot or
            cold. *(deals him stick blows)*

JOHNNY      *(attempts to protect himself from the blows).* Ouch! ouch!!
            ouch!!!

ANGELA      This will knock some sense into the dirty swine who used to
            tell when he was going to Lagos: *(mimicking Johnny)* "I have
            to go, I have to go, business is business!"

LORETTA     *(also dealing him stick blows).*  It's blows that this pig needs,
            whether on the head, on the back or on the rump!

JOHNNY      Ouch, ouch, ouch!

LORETTA     Angela, do you know he was telling me the same thing when
            he was going to Port Harcourt! 'Business is business!' *(giving
            him a last blow)* Be ashamed to have fooled me!

ANGELA      I'll damage some private parts of his body if the monster insists
            on not toeing the line! *(showing Johnny the door)* Now, out!
            So that in peace we may decide upon your fate!

JOHNNY      Right away! Little darling!

LORETTA     We must teach you a lesson that will percolate to all philander-
            ing males. *(escorting him to the door)* Now, out!

JOHNNY      Right away my love! *(he goes out)*

ANGELA      *(laughing).* Do you hear that?

LORETTA     *(mimicking Johnny).* "Right away little darling!" His "little
            darling" was so comical!

ANGELA      So was his "right away my love!"

LORETTA     How shall we deal with him? Your worthless husband!

ANGELA      Your deceitful fiance!

LORETTA     *(laughing)* My fiance!

ANGELA      It's better to laugh about it than cry!

LORETTA     A bit of humour won't do us any harm.

ANGELA First let's leave him to stew in his own juice.

LORETTA Let's make him curse himself for once.

ANGELA Will he remain a servant and a clown in your house?

LORETTA Outside the house, not in!

ANGELA Would you banish him like the plague?

LORETTA He's been postponing the date of the wedding under one pretext or the other. Let him keep doing that!

ANGELA Shall we see each other again?

LORETTA You will return to Port Harcourt and I will stay here! But you must come to me and I shall come to you.

ANGELA I don't at all hold you responsible for the disgraceful acts of my ... *(hesitating)* ex-husband. He has shamelessly exploited you and shamelessly deceived me! We are friends and shall remain friends.

LORETTA Friends for ever!

ANGELA I have an idea. It shall make us more than friends.

LORETTA I'm happy to hear that!

ANGELA It will allow us to have for ever under our thumb this little fellow who has duped us.

LORETTA I'm dying to hear of it!

ANGELA You become his second wife, thereby make this *de facto* situation an official one!

LORETTA His second wife! You his only wife suggesting this!

ANGELA In our tradition, for a man to take a second wife is a normal thing, so why do without it?

LORETTA I can scarcely say no to you.

ANGELA That way, our man will no longer have the chance to flirt from one woman to another! The butterfly will be pinned down. The migrating bird will be put in a cage, or rather in two cages, one in Lagos, your own, the other in Port Harcourt, mine! *(after a silence)* Well?

LORETTA      *(laughing).* That's well thought out, and well-calculated. Congrats! You have very good ideas my dear. As for my marriage to your crank of a husband, I accept it. Such a marriage does not scare me, far from it. We shall be two against one, two chicks who know the ropes against the only rooster whose spurs have been made blunt. In the farm-yard poultry, we are no stupid little geese!

ANGELA      Well said, my dear Loretta! Words flow from your lips with such ease that I should say they burst out of your lips! Let's improvise this farcical comedy as soon as possible. Let him be the court fool, with us as the queens!

LORETTA      We shall right now, at this very minute, convey to him the decision of the two managing women, half gorgon, half cerberus!

ANGELA      Those, though having no hair on their chins or above their lips ...

LORETTA      ... will make the little fellow toe the line ... the little fellow ...

ANGELA      ... so full of himself! Call him, Loretta! *(aside)* Loretta is a great lady!

LORETTA      I'll go, Angela! I'll call him. *(she goes out)*

ANGELA      I am getting chummy with Loretta, quite intimate too! We're ripe and ready to become bosom friends and co-wives!

LORETTA      *(coming back)* The little fellow is coming, gentle and docile as a lamb!

ANGELA      Let that bleating character wait for our goodwill behind the door! That will put an end to his conceit!

LORETTA      *(talking to Johnny who is behind the door before closing it)* Just wait. I'll call you. *(to Angela)* That certainly won't do him any harm.

ANGELA     Loretta, no more formality between us, agreed? Two sisters, that's what we are from now on, two sisters united against a common enemy!

LORETTA    Agreed, big sister!

ANGELA     Let him in now, he'll say amen to everything we say.

LORETTA    *(opening the door) (in a declamatory tone).* I'm opening the door for a doggie. It's a doggie that will enter!

JOHNNY     *(embracing them)* Yes, my darlings, I am all yours, at your service with all my heart. Ready to bark if you want me to!

ANGELA     *(pushing him back).* Enough of this gibberish which grates on my ears!

LORETTA    *(same acting)* Enough of that verbiage beyond comprehension!

ANGELA     Open wide your ears so that you don't miss even a word of our verdict shortly to be announced.

LORETTA    Piping hot from her mouth!

ANGELA     First of all, you, Mr. John Briggs, are sentenced to a three months' ban from staying in your marital and extra-marital homes.

           Secondly, at the end of the three months, you will marry Loretta Effiong here present.

JOHNNY     *(smiling and rubbing his hands together).* Oh, but that's great, that will make ...

ANGELA     *(roughly interrupting him).* Shut up! Who asked for your opinion?

JOHNNY     *(continuing)* Make an established fact official!

ANGELA     Shut up, I say! And don't think you'll be in paradise!

LORETTA    Oh not a chance!

ANGELA     We'll do everything  to see that your life is miserable and nearer hell than anything else!

JOHNNY   *(aside)* I 'm jumping out of the frying pan into the fire! Upon my word, these two shrews must have consulted each other, setting up that comedy beforehand. They're now as thick as thieves, though not so long ago, they could have scratched each other's eyes out. *(aloud)* But why so much cruelty, my darlings, since I've decided to behave myself, keep a low profile and comply with your least desires?

ANGELA   Your crimes cry out for vengeance, you should know.

LORETTA   Your shame proclaims you everywhere!

ANGELA   You considered us lower than dirt!

LORETTA   Trampling on our feminity!

ANGELA   It's time to act! Let's throw all his luggage on the landing. For three months let him go hang elsewhere. *(she opens the door and throws the luggage outside helped by Loretta)*

LORETTA   Three months hence let him return for the wedding.

JOHNNY   *(shattered and downcast).* From a frying pan into the fire!

*(and the curtain falls for a while and goes up again).*

. . .

## ACT VI

### SCENE IV

*The man arrives with the signboard indicating: PORT HARCOURT SIX MONTHS LATER. Johnny enters followed by Tony while the man leaves.*

JOHNNY   We can talk freely. Angela has left for the airport in the company of Loretta. But don't tell me any more about mistresses. Now I no longer have a minute to myself. I drift from one purgatory to another. I should have said hell! Each time I cross the Niger to go from Port Harcourt to Lagos or vice-versa, I have the feeling that I'm crossing the Styx.

TONY     Aren't you exaggerating?

JOHNNY     You can't imagine the way they keep watch over me, one in Port Harcourt, the other in Lagos, and I can hardly go and pee in peace! I even suspect that they have hirelings spying on me, my dear Tony. Oh my God, they've got their revenge and still they are satisfying their itch for vengeance!

TONY     But nevertheless, my dear Johnny *(making some suggestive gestures)* I know a young girl who would give you back a taste for life and take you to paradise!

JOHNNY     I don't have a minute to myself my poor Tony. They are always at my back.

TONY     Then cut into your business hours.

JOHNNY     *(interrupting him).* I am between the devil and the deep blue sea!

TONY     Cut into your business hours, better still, employ the girl proposed to you as a private secretary. That way you will always have her near you, ready to practise with you the very special gymnastics you're such an expert in! I saw you not so long ago with a girl on each knee!

JOHNNY     I must look twice before taking a third one.

TONY     Let me know your decision when you reach it.

JOHNNY     *(suddenly excited).* Say, is she beautiful?

TONY     No one could be more.

JOHNNY     Has the qualification of a personal secretary?

TONY     Oh yes, very personal indeed. She's got all the necessary paraphernalia. When it comes to love she's an expert! If I had to give her a degree I wouldn't give her a bachelor's but a master's degree!

JOHNNY    What about her brains.

TONY    Super! She can fool both your wives without batting an eyelid. Besides she speaks French.

JOHNNY    *(trying to speak French)* Oh Mademoiselle! *(blowing kisses with his fingers)* Je ... je t'aime, I love you! Tony! You, who's there before me like the tempter and who knows that I'll succumb at your mermaid-call, get away! *Vade Retro! Satana!*

TONY    O.K. I'm not the type to annoy you, you know.

JOHNNY    Better stay! I'm weak, and you know it. I'm ever ready to make the same mistakes!

TONY    When shall I introduce her?

JOHNNY    *(declaiming)* Go on Satan, carry on with your work! At the midday of my life, bring the girl to me, a not too innocent victim.

TONY    Your wishes are commands, dear brother! *(Tony and Johnny disappear, running, while the man with the signboard arrives. One can read: HIMALAYAS, TEN YEARS AFTER. Then he leaves while Johnny, looking appears walking slowly, dressed up as a bonze. He puts himself in a prayer position, immobile and indifferent to everything around him. The man with the signboard makes several appearances, his signboard alternately showing Port Harcourt and Lagos and different dates, while Loretta, Angela and Tony make numerous entries and exits that leave Johnny numb and dumb. Then Johnny stays alone on the scene).*

JOHNNY    *(smiling).* I've finally attained Nirvana, on the beautiful afternoon of my life *(raising his voice)* rid of all the demons including the one causing middle-age lust! I'm at last in paradise, *(shouting)* the only one, the true one, the paradise of John Briggs!

## THE END